TRAVEL WITH DOGS

● PET-FRIENDLY ACCOMMODATIONS ● HEALTH ● DOCUMENTATION

Contents

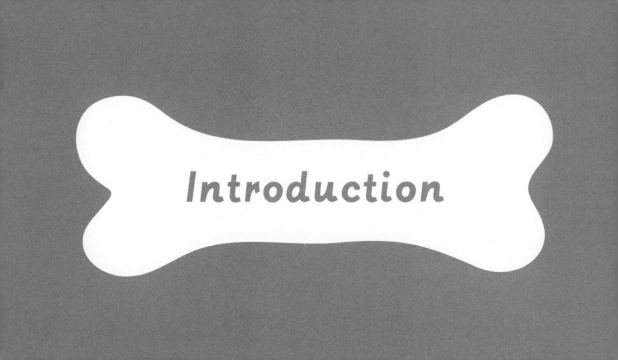

Introduction

In the pet industry, they're calling it a revolution. We are more and more likely to consider our pets as precious family members and these days when we go on holidays, our dogs come with us. No longer content to confine themselves to doggy environments like backyards and boarding kennels, pooches are hitting the skies, riding the waves and seeing the world as they vacation with their human companions.

And it's getting easier to take your pooch with you, wherever you go. Despite horror stories like the US Airways flight grounded after a terrier-on-the-loose bit a flight attendant, all the major US airlines allow pets on board. Pet-friendly accommodation is also booming, with hotel chains throwing in designer bedding, organic treats and in-house pet services from sitting to psychics in a bid for the growing doggy dollar.

If you prefer more down-to-earth vacations like road trips and camping, you'll find loads of state-of-the-art dog gear from sleeping bags to hiking boots, and online directories to help you choose your route and book your pet-friendly digs. And along the way you'll discover that many places – shops, tourist spots, even restaurants – will welcome your pooch with open arms and overflowing water bowls.

This book will tell you all you need to know about planning your doggy trip – from choosing your destination and finding places to stay, to canine health and travel documentation and, most importantly: how to make sure both you and your pooch have a great vacation. Let us go hand in paw to discover the brave new world of travel with dogs.

by Janine Eberle

Ready, set... Woof!

So you can't bear the thought of leaving your pooch at home when you set off on your next vacation. Good! He'll be as happy as a dog with two tails to be with you, and his companionship is sure to bring plenty of doggy joy to your trip.

Whether you want to take an all-out adventure hiking holiday or a culture vulture's city break, in the next state over or on the other side of the world, you can do it with your best furry friend trotting along at your side. He'll help you explore, he'll help you meet people, and you'll never suggest anything that he doesn't want to do!

But when you travel with Rover you can't leave things to chance, and there's a whole new set of things to think about and organize before you go. There's some work to do, but trust us – it's worth it!

Read on for an introduction to dog travel – all the way from cold wet snout to wagging tail.

The 10 best things about traveling with your dog

Dog travel is the best kind of travel, says self-confessed 'crazy dog lady' and one of our favorite dog bloggers, Kerry Martin. Here's why:

1. You see more when you explore on foot
You're more likely to get off the beaten track when you're exploring at dog level. And you'll slow down to take in the smells and sounds, as well as the sights.

2. You make new friends
Nothing helps you meet new people like having a dog. People say 'hello' and cross the road to pat your dog. You could get some great local tips and even organize a doggy play date!

3. Dogs make the most agreeable travel companions
Nothing you want to do on vacation will ever be a bad idea to your dog. A walk along the boardwalk? Woof! Brunch at the local café? Woof! A scenic hike? Woof! Picnic in the park? Woof!

4. You spend quality time with your pooch
In everyday life, you often don't spend the time that you'd like with your dog. When you travel together you get the time to do the things you both love.

5. Dogs make things more fun
The joy with which they approach any new experience is contagious, and so much fun to see. More laughter and more play are guaranteed.

6. You can travel with other dog lovers Your dogs have ready-made playmates and there's nothing more fun for dog-loving humans than sitting back laughing at their dogs' crazy antics.

7. You'll never be alone If you're a solo traveler, your dog means that you're never alone. You'll have a constant companion, and a great helper for meeting new people!

8. You go places you otherwise wouldn't Your dog will take you on unexpected detours. Marveling at the night sky on the last restroom break of the day, stumbling across a local bakery when you stop to break the drive… The little things you do for your pooch can become the highlights of your trip.

9. It's good for your dog Dogs need mental stimulation and they love new and interesting things. Racing through the snow or sniffing around an unfamiliar neighborhood exposes them to exciting new smells and sensations.

10. And it's good for you! Aside from the physical benefits of all that walking, spending time with your dog is good for your soul. Companionship, laughter, play, and snuggles make us happier – and there's more of all those things when we take a doggy vacation!

Read all about the adventures of Kerry and her dogs Keiko and Summer at www.puppytales.com.au.

What kind of trip?

What kind of traveler are you? Sophisticated big-city visitor? Adventurous outdoor explorer? Resort moocher? Rover can fit happily into any type of trip, but once you've decided to take him along, be prepared to adapt your trip to his doggy needs.

This book will give you some inspiration about different types of trips you can do, tell you what you need to consider, and help you to make your trip dog-friendly. The first things you should think about are:

• How are you getting there? If you're planning a road trip, long drives may need to be tackled more slowly than usual. If you're flying, there's lots of pre-planning needed to get Rover airborne. If he needs to travel in the hold of the plane, you should think about whether you're comfortable with that.

• Domestic or international? If you're traveling abroad, be prepared to spend some time researching and preparing your dog's travel documentation.

• Where will you stay? There are increasing numbers of dog-friendly accommodations out there, but you'll need to do your research before you go and you may have to make some compromises to find somewhere that will welcome your pooch.

Your dog will be happiest when he's out having adventures with you, not cooped up for long periods of time. If you want to take a road trip that involves long hours in the car, or a city break with lots of time in museums where he won't be welcome, think about what small adjustments you can make to turn it into a more dog-friendly trip. A road trip can be the perfect doggy vacation when it's broken

up by lengthy stops where you and Rover can get out to meet other dogs and get some exercise. A city break where you're able to take him with you most of the time (and can arrange doggy day-care for those times when you can't) can be a fantastic experience for both of you.

The important thing is to put plenty of thought into what you'll be doing on your trip, imagining how it will all work with your dog in the picture. Like what you see? Good! The next question is…

Is Rover up to it?

It's important that you honestly appraise how the reality of your dog fits in with your ideal trip. You don't want to find yourself on the road only to realize you've been unrealistic about your dog's ability to handle the kind of trip you want to take.

Your dog's age and fitness

You know what your dog's health and fitness levels are like. Make sure you take this into account when you're planning your itinerary.

Traveling with a pup? If you're flying, be sure that he's old enough to travel on an airplane (see p70). If you're traveling by car you'll need to train him to be a comfortable, happy passenger (see p32) . Make sure he's mastered basic training before you hit the road.

If your pooch is a senior citizen, he may not have the energy and stamina he once did – a multi-day hiking trip, for example, may be beyond him. Many hours in a cramped car might be too much for older, stiffer joints, and flying in the hold of an aircraft might be too stressful for your aged pooch.

Visit your vet before you start planning in earnest and discuss what kind of trip you're taking. Your vet

vet can help you understand the risks and limitations for your particular dog, discuss any health issues and help you plan vaccinations and health certification.

Your dog's temperament and behavior
Think of you and your dog as roving ambassadors for responsible dog travel. If you make a good impression out there in the wide world, travel with dogs will become easier and more welcome in the future.

• It's worth being brutal about this: don't consider traveling with a poorly-trained dog. Of course, all dogs have their moments and there aren't many perfect pooches out there. But your furry ambassador should have mastered basic obedience: sit, stay and recall at a minimum.

• You'll be meeting lots of new dogs and new people, so your dog must be well socialized and not aggressive. If you can't trust your dog not to growl or bark at new dogs, muzzle him. You might know that he would never bite, but the other dog's owner doesn't.

• If your dog gets separation anxiety, think carefully about the times when you might need to leave him alone, and what you will do to make sure he doesn't get anxious. Leaving a constantly barking dog at a campground or in a hotel room is not OK.

• Are long drives a part of your trip? If Rover isn't accustomed to spending time in the car, get him used to it by taking him on short drives and gradually increasing the duration.

• Take your dog on an overnight trip as practice, to introduce him to potentially anxiety-producing situations like sleeping in a new place with unfamiliar noises and smells.

• If your dog is able to sit peacefully and happily in a carrier or crate, it will make travel so much easier, whether on long drives, in the hold of an aircraft, or in a hotel room. That doesn't sound like your dog? Read on…

Learning to love the crate

If they're given a positive introduction to it, most dogs love their crate. Dogs are den animals and their natural instincts lead them to find solace in a safe, cozy haven. So for most dogs, crate training should come naturally.

Remember the cardinal rules of dog training: consistency and patience. And never, ever use the crate as punishment! A dog's crate should be their happy place.

• Make sure the crate is the right size: large enough for your dog to stand up, turn around, and lie down comfortably.

• Put a soft blanket and his favorite toy inside the crate.

• Place it in an area of the house where there's plenty of activity, so that he still feels a part of things.

• Sit on the floor next to the open crate and invite him in (using treats to tempt him if necessary). Continue this regularly until he is happy to walk into the crate.

• Start feeding him his meals in the crate, leaving the door open. This will create a positive association with the crate.

• Praise him whenever he enters the crate on his own.

The golden rules of doggy travel

Do your research Airline policies, dog-friendly accommodations, vet and dog-minding services… there's so much to find out! This book will help you make a list to check off as you go.

Get Rover ready Is he microchipped? Is he crate-trained? Is he comfortable with long drives? Does he need an obedience training top-up?

Plan well ahead Give yourself time to get vaccinations, organize documentation and do extra training. Book flights and make hotel or guesthouse reservations well in advance – dog places are often limited.

Visit your vet Always travel with a health certificate for your dog as proof that he's vaccinated and in good health. Discuss the planned trip and get your vet's advice.

Pack carefully Read our chapters on driving and flying with your dog and make sure you have everything he needs.

Plan fun! Put together an itinerary that includes plenty of things that you'll love doing together – hikes, beach play, exploring new neighborhoods…

Watch your pooch Constant change and new environments can make dogs anxious. Observe your dog and change course if he's over-tired or unwell.

Be a responsible dog owner Keep him on a leash when mandated, pick up his poop, don't let him growl at other dogs – just like you would at home, but with a higher level of care.

Keep it normal Keep your pooch on his regular feeding and walking times. Dogs love routine and keeping things normal will help him avoid anxiety.

• When you feel he's comfortable, start closing the door for short periods, increasing the time bit by bit.

• Once you're sure he's happy to be in the crate, lift it with him inside (get help if you need it!), gently jostle it, place it in the car, and drive around. This will prepare him for being lifted, loaded, and moved around when you travel.

If Rover is staying at home...

If you decide to leave your pooch at home, make sure he's well looked after. You want him to be happy, of course, but you also don't want to spend your whole trip worrying or feeling guilty!

A friend, especially a dog-owning one, is a great resource – even more so if you can return the favor when they want to go on vacation. Cultivate those dog-park friendships and always offer to look after the pooches of others if you can – create good doggy karma!

Another good option is to find a house-sitter who will look after your pet as well. This means Rover won't have the added stress of adapting to a new place – he'll be secure on his home turf, even if his beloved humans aren't there. This is especially worth considering if you have an older dog who may find a boarding kennel stressful, or a dog with separation anxiety who'll find it difficult to cope without you.

Finding a house-and-pet-sitter is made simple by services such as www.trustedhousesitters.com; hunt out local house-sitting services too.

Choosing a boarding kennel

In our world of pampered pets, dog boarding is a growth industry. Pooch palaces and luxury doggy resorts boasting five-star amenities are popping up around the world, with professional handlers, aromatherapy shampooing, and around-the-clock webcams so you can check in on your woofer 24/7 to reassure yourself that he's having an even better time than you are.

Whether you're going for super-luxe or down-to-earth digs, the best way to find a good kennel is by word of mouth. Ask your dog-park friends, your vet and your dog-groomer for recommendations. Then visit your shortlisted kennels and evaluate them carefully.

Is the facility clean and well kept? Look for raised beds so your dog isn't sleeping on a hard floor.

Observe the staff. Are they interacting well with the animals? Do they seem to enjoy their work?

And the dogs: are they relaxed, comfortable, sleeping? That's a good sign. Dogs who look anxious and are pacing or barking isn't.

The space should include outdoor areas to play and socialize, plus multiple rest spots, inside and out.

Ask about food. What type of food will your dog be fed, and how often?

Ask about exercise. How often will he have access to an exercise area? Is it shared, and how does the staff ensure that dogs are socializing happily?

What happens if Rover gets sick? What's their procedure for contacting you, and for contacting a vet?

Find out if you can pay extra for walks, grooming or other treats so your dog gets a little extra attention.

Did they ask about your dog? They should want to know about his particular needs or behavior so they can make him as comfortable as possible.

If the kennel is unwilling to give you a full tour, seems to be in disrepair or doesn't require proof of vaccination, steer clear.

If you're off on a longer trip, it's a good idea to give your dog a couple of short stays at the kennel before you set off to see how he copes. It will also give you an opportunity to evaluate the standard of care.

School vacations, Thanksgiving, Christmas, and long weekends are very busy times and some places will book out months in advance. Book early, or avoid peak times.

On the road

So you want to go roving with Rover? Watch miles of open road disappear underneath your wheels while your pooch pants along in the back seat, patiently awaiting the chance to lift his leg on a different type of grass and sniff the thrilling scents of a different type of air...

Road trips make great doggy vacations. You can control when you travel and when you rest, you don't have the stress of transporting Rover by airplane, and no matter where you live, you're sure to have some very dog-pleasing destinations an easy drive away.

While doggy car travel is relatively easy, you can't just toss Rover in back and hit the road. There are some things you should do before you go to ensure stress-free fun times for all concerned – both dog and human. Consider how your woofer feels about car travel, plan ahead (and train ahead if necessary), make sure you have the right gear, and prepare for some cross-country doggy adventure.

Getting ready to hit the road

While it might be perfectly acceptable for us humans to set off half-cocked on a spontaneous road trip, as soon as dogs are involved, pre-planning becomes crucial. Here's what you should think about before you hit the road.

May I see some ID? An up-to-date microchip registration is the best way to make sure you can find Rover if he absconds. And make sure he's always wearing his tags with your current phone number.

Visit your vet Check that your dog's vaccinations are up-to-date, and ask if he needs additional shots (for example, in some areas of the US he may need a vaccination against Lyme disease). It's a good idea to travel with proof of rabies vaccinations, as campgrounds and accommodations may ask to see them.

Plan your route Include rest stops (see p28) and note the details of emergency vet facilities along the route and at your destination.

Book ahead You can't take a free-and-easy approach to accommodations, as Rover won't be welcome everywhere. Research pet-friendly places to stay (see p84) and book well ahead.

Research your trip Will your pooch be allowed into that national park or attraction you plan to visit? If not, you'll need to investigate day-care services.

Pack a bag for Rover

Make sure that you've got everything that your pooch is going to need en route and at your destination.

Collar, leash and ID tag Make sure he wears them even in the car, in case there's an incident and he runs away from you.

Food, water and bowls Bring plenty of water for the drive, and supplies of the food that your dog is used to – this is not the time to experiment with Rover's diet.

Treats, chews and toys To keep him happy and occupied.

Paper towels, washcloths and cleaning supplies For the inevitable accidents and grubby moments.

Poop bags For rest stops and anywhere else you venture.

Blankets Take things that smell like home to help keep your dog relaxed wherever he is.

Doggy first aid kit Get a good first-aid manual (book or app) and assemble a DIY first-aid kit, starting with gauze pads, tape, bandage rolls and scissors, antiseptic, hydrogen peroxide (to induce vomiting – only when directed by a vet), thermometer, sterile saline solution, and tweezers.

Doggy car safety

If your dog vacation fantasy involves cruising the open road, Rover hanging his head out the window with jowls flapping in the breeze – forget it. He might enjoy it, but it's unsafe for both of you. He must be well restrained – both to protect him in case of an accident, and to stop him from attempting to give you (the driver) an ill-timed lick on the face. In many places, free-range dog driving is strongly frowned upon and you may be fined if you're pulled over with a freelance dog in the car.

Of course, you should *never* drive with a dog in your lap. It's not advisable for your pooch to travel in the front seat, either – it's distracting for the driver, and the dog could be injured by a deployed airbag.

Crate travel

Crates are the safest option, if the size of your dog or your car is not a limiting factor. An added benefit is you'll be able to use the crate at your destination too, whether you're staying at a hotel, campsite or luxury resort.

If your pooch isn't already crate-trained, it should be fairly easy to get him accustomed to it – see p14 for crate-training advice.

The crate should be large enough that your dog can stand up completely and turn around, but not so large that he can slide around inside when you swerve to avoid a cat/moose/pedestrian. It's important that the crate is securely fastened in place so that it can't move around in the car.

There are soft-sided collapsible crates for easy storage, and crates on wheels to help with transport.

The crate you choose should be well-ventilated and structurally sound – look for crates produced with strict quality guidelines.

If your dog is older or you're concerned about his mobility, consider getting a ramp or steps to help him climb in and out of the car with ease.

Harnesses and restraints

A harness fastened to a seat belt is the equivalent of a human seat belt for woofers. It gives your pooch some freedom, but he can't roam around the vehicle, and he won't become a furry projectile if there's a crash.

There are no real safety regulations in the pet industry, and recent crash tests have shown that many of the harnesses out there don't provide adequate protection in the event of a crash. Do your research: read product reviews and make sure you're buying a

quality product – without wanting to be too melodramatic, your dog's life may depend on it.

Be sure that you use a strong, good-quality harness, and that your dog is held fairly firmly in place (he should be able to stand up, but not move around too much). Make sure the clips and straps are sturdy and that the harness won't unclip if your dog steps on the release button.

To make bigger dogs more comfortable in the back seat, it's possible to get a deck or shelf that fits over the seat, creating a secure flat area that they can spread out on (while wearing their harness, of course).

Barriers

A barrier can be a good option if you have a bigger dog and a bigger car with a flat area at the back. It creates a little caged-off area that your dog can move around in, while being prevented from flying around the car if you have to brake suddenly.

Be sure that the barrier you select can be securely attached to the car's interior and that it's solid enough to take the weight of your dog in an accident. And be aware that while your pooch might be happy with the greater movement it allows, the barrier isn't as effective in securing him in the event of an accident. The trunk is usually the car's crumple zone, so it's dangerous if you're rear-ended, and even in a minor accident the door could open and Rover could run onto the road.

Driving safety tips

Turn off your power windows Your dog could accidentally open the window and jump out. Or he could manage to get his head stuck or some other crazy dog-like stunt, which is sure to distract you while you're driving.

Don't bake your dog Never leave your dog alone in a car on a hot (or even just warm) day. The temperature inside a car is exponentially higher than the outside temperature, and your dog can suffer brain damage or die in a very short time. Very cold weather is equally dangerous.

No jowls in the breeze It's cute, but it's not safe. Don't let your dog hang his head out the window – you could be driving straight to the vet if a stone is kicked up into his eye. And riding unrestrained in an open truck bed is also a no-no.

Keeping Rover happy and comfortable

Dogs thrive on routine. To keep him relaxed as you travel, try to keep to your dog's normal feeding timetable. Ideally, give him a light meal at his normal time three to four hours before you leave. He might snack during the drive, but don't feed him a full meal until you've arrived at your destination and it is his normal feeding time.

It's a good idea to take your dog for a short walk ten or 15 minutes before you set off, which will give him a burst of feel-good hormones to keep him calm on the trip.

Gnawing and chewing can help your dog relax, and keep him quiet while you are concentrating on driving the car. Give your pooch his favorite chew toy or a bone or bully stick to keep him happy and occupied.

Make sure the car is well ventilated with open windows or air-conditioning and is not too hot or too cold. Consider buying shade screens for the windows to keep your dog out of the sun if he'll be in the back seat.

If your dog get anxious, the sound of your voice will calm him – but don't over-soothe him, as that may send an unintentional signal that he has something to be afraid of. Some people also swear by playing soothing music – it can't hurt, and it might be good for both of you!

Doggy pitstops

Stop regularly – for at least 15 to 30 minutes every three or four hours – so he can relieve himself, burn off some pent-up energy and get a little mental stimulation. It will be much more enjoyable for both of you if you plan ahead to make your pitstops somewhere pet-friendly, even if it's just a little dog park so you can take a decent walk. It's no fun walking around the carpark of a freeway-side roadhouse.

Offer him some water (bring water from home –

you don't want strange water to result in a tummy upset when you still have hours of travel ahead) and give him some affection when you stop. You might give him a small snack, but avoid feeding him a full meal until you reach your destination.

Coping with car sickness

Puppies are more susceptible to motion sickness than full-grown dogs, just as children are more likely to suffer it than adults. This is because the ear structures used for balance aren't yet fully developed in young dogs (or humans). Happily, most dogs outgrow it, but some become conditioned to equate travel with vomiting, even after their ears have fully matured. Some dogs may suffer car-related anxiety related to an unpleasant association – see p32 for tips on reconditioning your dog to cope with car travel.

You'll know if your dog is experiencing motion sickness if he shows signs of uneasiness. Look for yawning, whining, and drooling, or he may just seem listless. Of course, if he vomits you'll know he's not feeling great.

To help with your pooch's queasiness, make sure you're doing all you can to keep him happy and comfortable (see p27). Also:

Face him forward so he sees less movement. Looking out of the side windows creates a blur, which can cause or exacerbate motion sickness.

Avoid keeping him in the back seat, where there is the most motion.

Open the windows a crack to reduce air pressure and allow better ventilation.

Try crating your dog to stop him from looking outside too much.

Keep it cool – a hot, stuffy car can make car sickness worse.

Holistic treatments can be effective. Ginger and peppermint are often recommended for nausea, and valerian or a pet rescue remedy for anxiety may be worth trying.

Medications are available, but consider them a last resort and speak to your vet before trying them.

If your dog vomits, don't pull over to clean it, as this will signal to him that puking stops the car. Ignore it and clean it after he's out of the car. If you get upset, he may associate your emotional response with the car and this may increase his car travel stress.

Rental car policies

If you are planning a fly-drive trip with a furry traveling companion, the news is good: most rental car firms are pet friendly. However, there are a few things you should be aware of:

• **Confirm with the rental company that they do allow dogs and if any restrictions apply, before you confirm your reservation and go to pick up the car.**

• **Some companies may insist that you travel with your dog in a crate or carrier.**

• **Most policies will state that there will be additional charges if extra cleaning is required – something to consider if your dog is a heavy shedder.**

• **You will be liable if your dog causes any damage to the car, and this is unlikely to be covered by standard insurance.**

• **Place an old blanket or waterproof sheet over the seat to protect it from claws and teeth, reduce the amount of hair left in the car, and mitigate any accidents.**

• **If your dog is a chewer, make sure he has toys or chew sticks to distract him from the rental car's novel and tempting leather upholstery.**

31

Training your dog to like the car

If your dog is very scared or anxious about being a passenger, all is not lost. It's possible to train him to like riding in the car, but as with all dog training it's all about consistency and persistence. It might take weeks or even longer, but you can help reduce your dog's anxiety by following these steps. Take it slowly, and don't move onto the next step until you've both mastered the previous one.

1. Let him explore the car from the outside. Let him walk around and sniff it, and reward him with treats or his favorite toy. Praise him and keep your voice upbeat.

2. Sit in the car with the engine off. Get him to play or just sit quietly and reward him with treats.

3. Sit in the car with the engine running but don't go anywhere. Sit at the wheel and have your dog sit where he'll be sitting when you drive. It's OK to distract him with treats or toys.

4. Take short drives around your neighborhood. Visit a park or a pet store – make sure your destination is one that he'll be happy about (or at least, not one he hates, like the groomer or the vet!).

5. Steadily make longer trips and remember that the more frequently you do these steps, the quicker your dog will become conditioned to like – or at least tolerate – traveling in the car.

RVing and Camping

What could be more dog-friendly than a big kennel on wheels? Many dog owners swear by the RV (or caravan) for their doggy vacations. In fact, according to the Recreational Vehicle Industry Association, 61 percent of RVers travel with pets, and 90 percent of those pets are dogs (because why would you bother traveling with a cat? Woof!).

Campground life can be paradise for pooches and their human traveling companions, as long as you plan ahead and make sure your homes away from home (and kennels away from kennel) are welcoming to dogs. You're sure to find little friends for your pooch in your new temporary neighborhoods, and he'll help you sniff out new friends for you, too.

If you want to strike out and hit some hiking trails, taking Rover along will only enhance the experience. He should do his bit and carry his own gear, of course – and what could be more adorable than a dog wearing a backpack?

Hitting the road in a mobile home

As with any poochie holiday, planning ahead is paramount. Plan your route, including rest stops, and make sure you know what veterinary facilities are along the way (see p22 for more planning tips).

Make sure you've researched all the campgrounds you intend to stay at, confirming that they are dog friendly and, specifically, that they're friendly towards *your* dog. Some allow only small dogs, some limit the number of dogs you can bring in, and some forbid 'aggressive breeds' (the definition of which may differ campground by campground).

Find out if there are facilities at the campground for doggy 'day-care' – kennels where your dog can be looked after when you're out for the day. If not, are there local boarding kennels nearby that offer day boarding? If you're planning to spend time visiting places Rover isn't welcome, you'll need to research this carefully before you go.

Is your dog a camper?

Think about how your dog will fit into campground life. He should have basic obedience training – be able to come when called, sit when asked, and not jump on people. If there are any behavioral issues that could aggrieve fellow campers, you'll need to deal with them before you set out. Ask yourself:

• Is Rover well socialized? He'll be meeting lots of new people and other dogs at the campground. If he doesn't like strangers or get along with other dogs, that could be a problem.

• Is he a barker? That will be an issue when you're staying in close quarters with other campers.

• **Does he like sleeping inside, in close quarters with you? (And, by the way, how do you feel about it?!)**

• **Is your dog very excitable? Does he have a high prey drive? Being outdoors is highly stimulating and it can be overwhelming and even frightening for dogs that aren't used to it. Dogs such as terriers, which were bred to hunt, can become uncontrollable when potential prey is around – consider how wound-up your dog will become in close proximity to thrilling wildlife.**

• **If he's not used to it, take some time to get your dog accustomed to being tied up while you're nearby, to simulate what it will be like when you're camping. If you're planning on crating him, he'll need to be crate-trained if he's not already (see p14).**

Campground life with dogs

Travel is generally stressful for dogs, and it may take your pooch a while to get used to the roaming RV lifestyle. Take note of these tips to help you both settle in for the ride.

Chow time It's a good idea to bring along a full supply of his usual food – he may be more sensitive to change than normal. Otherwise, make sure his regular brand is a healthy, widely available brand that you're sure to be able to find at chains or big-box pet suppliers.

Be predictable Dogs love routine. Try to keep meals, exercise, and treats at similar times each day. It will help you if he has regular potty breaks, and he'll be calmer knowing what to expect.

Keep him active A tired dog is a good dog. Depending on your dog's breed and personality he

may need a good extended sniff around, a run, or a game of fetch. If he's not coming with you on your hike or day trip, make sure he gets some dedicated time for exercise and mental stimulation every day.

Set boundaries early If you want to limit your dog's roaming rights in your rig (for example, to keep the bedroom area off-limits), enforce it consistently right from the beginning. You'll find that much easier than to recondition a dog who's used to roaming freely.

Make friends! Nurture mutually beneficial relationships with other dog-loving campers. You can trade favors by watching each others' dogs if you want to go out for the day somewhere they can't go along.

Take care in hot weather Don't leave your dog in the RV on hot days if you want to go exploring and you can't take your dog with you. Even if you have

air-conditioning, there is the risk of a malfunction or power outage. Don't let Rover bake!

Safety on the road Between campgrounds, the same rules apply as for car travel. Rover shouldn't roam free while you're in motion – he must travel in a secured crate or wear a dog seatbelt. Never let him ride alone in a camper that you're hauling – it can be a rocky ride back there, and it may get too hot or too cold. He needs to be in the same vehicle as you, crated or restrained.

Campground etiquette

It's super important that your dog is a good campground citizen – we travelers with pooches don't want to get a bad name and lose our camping rights! Remember that some people just don't like dogs. You'll need a quiet, well behaved, and obedient dog to win them over and make a success of the RV lifestyle. If that's not what you have, start working on it now!

Be on poop patrol at all times – always have poop bags with you and dispose of your dog's waste responsibly. Watch where he urinates – never let him go near someone else's camp area.

Keep him leashed well away from the traffic areas and your campfire, and be sure to keep an eye on him to make sure he's not getting tangled around tent poles, stakes, chairs, trees, etc.

Consider bringing a doggy playpen – a portable enclosure will give him a bit more freedom.

Supervise your dog Even if your dog is well socialized and trained, he'll be under stress and in unfamiliar surroundings, and he may act unpredictably. When you're busy setting up and packing up, make sure you take the time to secure him.

Talk to your neighbors You may not be aware that Rover is barking constantly when you are out for the day – but your fellow campers certainly are! Encourage them to let you know if your pooch is misbehaving while you are out. It will break the ice with them and get the relationship off to a good start – that could be important if Rover destroys their vacation peace and you need to smooth things over with them!

Take him with you If your pooch is barking constantly while you're out, take him with you wherever you go, find a fellow camper to look after him while you're away, or put him in day-care.

Healthy hiking dogs

Of course, as for any travel, your dog should be up-to-date on all his vaccinations (including rabies). He should be microchipped and have your current contact information on his collar tags.

Do your research into hazards you might encounter on the trail. If Lyme disease is endemic to the area, consider getting him vaccinated.

Don't feed your dog a large meal before the hike. Give him snacks and small meals along the way, but keep full meals for when you stop for the day or get home.

Use sunscreen on exposed skin if your dog has a light coat or light colored nose. Pay special attention to the nose and tips of the ears.

Don't let him drink from standing water – it can harbor harmful, even fatal, parasites and bacteria.

Keep a keen eye for other animals, broken glass and debris, and rocky terrain. Any cuts or scrapes should be attended to straight away.

Dehydration and heat exhaustion is a risk in warmer months (and hypothermia in colder months). Stop for water breaks often, and slow down if your dog seems to be breathing heavily. Look out for excessive panting and drooling, stumbling, or disorientation. If your dog has any of these symptoms, stop immediately and take a break until he has recovered.

Check your dog over carefully when you get home to look for ticks, insect, or spider bites, scrapes and other wounds. Pay particular attention to the footpads and between the toes, and in, under, and around the ears.

On the hiking trail with Rover

Hitting the trail and exploring the great outdoors with your dog can be incredibly rewarding. And for your dog, being active and enjoying nature with his best friend – what could be better?

Before embarking on a multi-day hike, consider your dog's age, health, and personality. Is he physically ready to take on a long hike? It's a good idea to check with your vet how much exercise he should be able to handle. Just like you need a training regime before tackling a challenging hike, your dog does too! Ease him into it with shorter hikes before taking on the big one.

Will your dog be calm and manageable when other people or pooches pass by? Does he come when called, no matter how enticing the distraction? If not, you won't be able to protect him from beasties he encounters when he's off-leash. You don't want a dog with a face full of porcupine quills or a snakebite, miles away from anywhere.

• **Check the regulations for the areas you'll be hiking in. For example, most US national parks don't allow dogs to share the trail. In many cases they need to be on-leash.**

• **If Rover gets injured on the trail, it will be up to you to take care of him. Be first-aid ready with a well-prepared kit (see p23), and consider taking a dog first-aid class before you go.**

• **Research water sources along your route. And remember that your dog may need to eat more, as he'll probably be exerting himself more than usual – check with your vet and be sure to pack enough food.**

• **It's ideal if your dog can carry his own food and**

water. If you're in a leave-no-trace area, he should also carry out his own waste. (Otherwise, dispose of it just as you would your own – at least 200 feet away from trails, camps, and water sources, with biodegradable bags.)

Doggy hiking gear

Just like you need to kit yourself out for a big hike, Rover needs his own gear too. Consider the terrain, the length of the hike, and the weather – what do you need to bring to be sure that he is safe, comfortable, and manageable on the trail?

Leash You may want to consider a waistbelt system or a leash you can clip to your pack, to keep your hands free. Some public trails specify the leash should be less than six feet long.

Dog packs are little backpacks for dogs that will allow them to carry their own supplies. Generally speaking, dogs can carry up to 25 percent of their body weight. Build up to this gradually, get your dog accustomed to carrying the pack, and be sure it's properly fitted before you go.

Travel bowls You can get collapsible bowls made of silicone or canvas – the silicone ones are generally more durable and easier to clean.

Sleeping gear will depend on how cold it will be on your hike and how cold-tolerant your dog is. You might want to share a two-person bag with your dog, get a kiddie sleeping bag for him, or buy a special dog sleeping bag.

Dog clothing might be necessary if the conditions are harsh – perhaps a jacket to keep your dog warm in the cold, and boots to protect his paw pads on harsh terrain, be it rocky, icy, or burning hot.

Seeing the world

As the world becomes increasingly more connected, both physically and virtually, it's easier than ever to explore the world beyond your own backyard, whether it's on a short trip or as a permanent lifestyle choice. And there's no need to leave your furry friend at home. With a bit of planning, you and poochie could become global nomads!

But there's plenty to consider before you set off. As Johnny Depp and his jet-setting Yorkies famously discovered when they tried to bypass Australian quarantine, there are different rules for different countries. These rules are strictly enforced, and the consequences of flouting them can be severe for human and canine alike.

It can be a dog-eat-dog world out there with entry regulations, 'pet passports,' rabies vaccinations, and more – here's your doggy globe-trotting checklist.

Passport for pooches

The pet passport came into being as part of the European Union Pet Travel Scheme (PETS). PETS was initially introduced to enable animals to travel more freely between the UK and other EU countries. Now, the term 'pet passport' is used more loosely for the collection of documents your pet needs to enter any given country.

It allows you to group all the vital information about your pet in one place, making it straight-forward for border officials to verify your pet's health and vaccinations and avoid, or at least minimize, quarantine.

The key thing to remember is that outside the EU, countries still have differing regulations. There are, however, a couple of basic rules that are common to all countries:

- **Microchipping (to international specifications)**
- **Certified rabies vaccination, with a specified time period after vaccination, or other evidence of effectiveness (such as a blood test). The time period varies between countries; for the UK, for example, it's three weeks.**

Countries may also have varying requirements for tick, flea, and tapeworm treatments, or they might require additional or different documentation. There may be limited ports into which animals can arrive – don't just assume that Rover can disembark the plane in the same place you do!

The moral of the story is this: it's vital to check what the specific requirements are for the countries you are traveling between. Do this in good time before you are due to travel. For example, if you're bringing your

dog to Australia – a country with particularly stringent requirements – it's recommended that you start the process six months before you and Rover are due to arrive.

And remember – you'll also need to meet the specific requirements for your own country to bring your dog back home.

Your vet can help to create a passport for your dog, or you can use a resource such as www.pettravelstore.com, which clearly lists requirements for each country (and, for a small fee, will send you a pack of the documentation you need for your travel).

Rabies and quarantine

While it horrified dog lovers the world over, the Australian government's threat to euthanize Johnny Depp's Yorkies can be better understood if you see Boo and Pistol not as beloved pets, but as a serious biohazard.

Australia, along with New Zealand, Iceland, and Japan, is one of only a handful of countries classified as rabies-free. That explains its particularly strict requirements – as well as the necessary vaccinations, tests, and documents, all dogs spend at least 10 days in an Australian quarantine facility (luckily for Oz-bound doggies this has changed recently from a minimum of 30 days!). Other rabies-free countries have similar rules, as does Hawaii, the only US state with rabies-free status.

The countries of the world are divided into three classifications: rabies-free, rabies-controlled, and high-rabies. Before your dog starts jet-setting, you need to know the rabies classification of your starting point and destination, as well as any countries you'll be passing through.

If your dog does have to spend time in quarantine, be aware that you'll need to pay for this service,

and you may need to arrange it yourself and book it ahead of time. It's also likely to limit the ports through which you're able to enter the country, and you probably won't be able to visit him while he's there. Do your homework and start the process well in advance.

Other medical questions

While rabies is by far the most important health consideration for dogs traveling internationally, there are other health issues that need to be considered. For example:

- **When traveling into the UK, you'll need to show in your documentation that your dog has been treated for tapeworm within the last five days.**
- **Dogs traveling from the US to Australia will need to prove they've had their canine flu shots.**
- **If you're traveling from or through the Malaysian peninsula you may need proof that your dog hasn't had contact with pigs for the last 60 days.**
- **If a tick or flea is found on your dog coming into Australia or New Zealand, be prepared for a drastically extended and expensive quarantine.**

There are many additional medical requirements that are subject to constant change. If your travel is complex or you're traveling to a country with stringent requirements, consider using a professional pet shipping agent in your home country to help figure out what documentation you need to organize, arrange tests and treatments, and source suitable flights and transport. Some airlines require a pet exporter to book flights for animals to avoid troubles that may lead to delayed flight departures. See p63 for more.

The world's most dog-friendly places

The results are in, and they show that Europeans love their dogs more than the rest of us. Or at least, they're happier to treat their dogs like humans. In many European countries, you'll find dogs enjoying cafés, shopping malls and the subway.

The love of the *French* for their dogs is legendary, and more charming now that its dark side – Paris' poopy sidewalks – is being addressed. Dogs are welcome in restaurants, bars, and shops – almost anywhere humans go – and you'll see them walking off-leash, along busy *rues* everywhere.

While some travelers claim that *Italians* love dogs more than anyone else, dogs in *Switzerland*, *Belgium*, *Germany*, *Austria*, *Hungary*, and *Slovenia* also take their walks on easy street. Would-be Swiss dog owners must complete a course on animal understanding before they're allowed to get a pooch, and there are strict rules about training, including a ban on electric collars.

In the *USA* and *Canada*, as well as *Australia* and *New Zealand*, there are many open spaces and it's easy to find off-leash areas (though national parks are often on-lead). But dogs are generally seen as outside creatures. They aren't welcome inside restaurants, bars, cafés, etc (although your dog may be able to sit with you in an outside area).

There's a similar attitude in the *UK*, with the notable exception of London's Underground, where dogs are welcome – with the proviso that you carry them on the escalators in case they injure their paws! There's even an Instagram hashtag to prove it: check out #dogsonthetube.

Cruising canines

For luxury trans-Atlantic travel, there's Cunard's *Queen Mary 2*, the only cruise ship that welcomes dogs. And it's quite a welcome.

While dogs aren't allowed in the staterooms or any public areas, they rule on Deck 12, where they're free to roam on their own private deck, sniffing the sea air and making friends. As of a refit in 2016, there are 22 private kennels – always booked out.

A full-time kennel master tends to the pack and keeps the deck sparkling. There are set visiting times, but if you want to spend more time with your pooch, it can be arranged. As for safety, have you ever seen a dog in a life jacket? Adorable! There's one for every dog, plus a staff member is assigned to each pooch in case of an emergency.

Dogs have been sailing in style with Cunard since Liz Taylor's poodle cruised in the 1950s, and there's still a scent of celebrity around the doggy guests. The dog deck is a tourist attraction for non-dog-owning cruisers, and on photo day your dog gets dressed up in a gorgeous little *QM2* jacket, you and the kennel-master put on your formal outfits, and you're snapped for an official cruise souvenir photo.

The *QM2* travels between New York City, Hamburg and Southampton. The dog fare is US$800 to US$1000, depending on size. Not all breeds are accepted – very large dogs, like Great Danes and breeds banned in the UK, like pit bulls, aren't welcome. The kennels are very popular and you may need to organize vaccinations and documentation – start the booking process 12 months in advance. See www.cunard.com for more.

Is your dog welcome?

Many countries have imposed bans on particular breeds of dogs, in the belief that these dogs are prone to aggression and can be dangerous. It's a fraught issue for dog lovers – most animal welfare organizations, including the ASPCA, believe it unfairly targets breeds instead of irresponsible owners. For owners of these breeds, it can make travel (domestic as well as international) difficult.

There are a hotchpotch of bans in place internationally, with the American pit bull terrier, American Staffordshire terrier and Staffordshire bull terrier the most commonly banned. The dogo Argentino, rottweiler and tosu inu are banned by a number of countries, while among the Ukraine's 80 banned breeds are some surprising inclusions like Welsh and fox terriers and Labrador retrievers.

In the USA, there aren't countrywide bans but rather a jigsaw of local restrictions. Most commonly banned are the pit bull breeds cited above. Often, any breed that appears to be a pit bull mix is subject to bans, regardless of whether it has bully genes. But other breeds can be affected, including bulldogs, mastiffs, and even non-bully breeds like chow chows, Doberman pinschers, and dalmatians.

Don't take your dog to a country or city where it's completely banned – you risk having it confiscated and even euthanized – and if regulations are in place be prepared to muzzle your dog or comply with other restrictions. The best way to find out what the restrictions are is to contact local animal control offices.

And don't just assume your dog is OK – to the Ukrainian authorities, your lovable Airedale may seem a terrifying, bloodthirsty killer!

Flying with dogs

Things didn't go so well for Laika, the world's first flying dog. After she was catapulted into orbit by the Russian space program in 1957, details of her fate become sketchy. Suffice to say, she never made it back to her earthbound kennel. Nowadays, our furry friends routinely make it to 30,000 to 40,000ft (standard cruising altitude for passenger planes) and come out happy as Lassie on the other side.

It's becoming ever easier and more pleasant for dogs to fly, with more and more airports providing dog-friendly facilities and airlines catering better to pooches and the humans that accompany them. Some airlines, like Virgin and JetBlue, even let you earn frequent flyer points for doggy travel!

But it's not all bones and jerky. Depending on where you're going (and the size of your dog), it can be a pretty complicated business to get your dog airborne. So what do you need to do if you want to take to the skies with your pooch?

Before you hit the runway

While the Humane Society and the ASPCA advise against taking dogs on a plane (especially if they're traveling in the hold), it's also true that many thousands of pets fly every year, and incidents are relatively rare (although they do happen). All travel involves risk, and your role as Rover's human is to assess that risk for him – is he better off coming with you than staying home? Knowing his health and temperament, and what kind of flight you're embarking on, how do you think he will cope with it?

Where will your dog ride? Generally speaking, in the US and Europe it's common for smaller dogs to be allowed to travel in the cabin with you, but if Rover is over 15lbs (7kg), he'll probably be too big. In other countries including the UK, Australia, and New Zealand, all dogs (except assistance dogs) travel in the hold. It's worth noting that many experts recommend that you should avoid transporting your dog in this way unless absolutely necessary.

How long is the flight? Are there layovers or connections involved? The shorter the flight, the less stressful it will be for your pooch.

How much will it cost? All airlines have pet fees, which can vary widely – as a rule of thumb, for domestic flights in the US, expect to pay around $100 for in-cabin flights and $200 plus for flights where your dog rides in the hold.

Whether squished under the seat or alone in a strange, loud baggage hold, the flight is not going to be a bundle of fun for Rover. A tough, unflappable dog who loves being in his crate or carrier may take the unpleasant experience in his stride; but if your dog is fearful, nervous; or suffers from separation anxiety and you know in your heart of hearts he's going to be beside himself, consider truthfully whether it's worth it.

Which airline?

Airlines are not all created equal when it comes to transporting pets – some are pet-friendlier than others. Do some research: visit forums (travel forums like TripAdvisor, or dog forums like www.pettravel.com/forum) to learn from the experiences of other dog owners.

Be aware that airlines have a variety of restrictions on transporting animals. Some of the different regulations are outlined below – before you book, be sure you fully understand what restrictions apply to your flight and your pooch.

- **Airlines may refuse to carry particular breeds in the hold, for example, snub-nosed dogs (like boxers and pugs), as they have difficulty breathing at altitude (see p70).**
- **There are likely to be specific rules about the type of carrier your dog needs to be in, whether it's flying in the cabin or the hold.**
- **For flights with connections, you should understand what will happen at the transit point. Will you have to claim and re-check your dog? (Very likely yes, if you're traveling on different airlines.)**
- **You may not be allowed to travel with your dog if the temperature is either extremely hot or extremely cold at any location on your itinerary (see p68).**
- **There may be a limit to the number of animals accepted on each flight – contact the airline early to reserve a place for your pooch.**

If Rover is in the cabin with you

If you have a mini-pooch, and the airline you're flying with allows him to travel in the cabin, rejoice! This will generally be a far less stressful way for both of you to fly. However, there are still a number of rules and regulation involved. They differ slightly from airline to airline, but they'll go something like this:

• His carrier should be around 8–10in (20–25cm) high, 12–13in (30–33cm) wide and 17–23in (43–58cm) long (exact measurements vary by airline). Your dog should be able to stand up, turn around, and lie down comfortably.

• The carrier must fit under the seat in front of you, and it must be stowed there for take-off and landing (and sometimes throughout the entire flight).

• It must have a waterproof bottom and allow for adequate ventilation.

• Soft-sided carriers are a good option, as they can be squished down, with your dog lying down to fit under the seat in front, while allowing more space at other times.

• The carrier will generally count as your carry-on baggage allowance (with most airlines, that means you'll only be able to bring one small additional piece on board).

• During the flight, you can move your dog's carrier out so it is under your feet. On some airlines, you can lift the carrier onto your lap, but he can't come out of the carrier. You can't even allow his head to stick out (but you can put your hand in to give him a pat or a treat).

Make sure your pooch is familiar with and happy in his carrier well before you fly (see p14 on how to train your dog to love his carrier).

Line the carrier with a good absorbent pad, and throw in his favorite soft toy. Put in his leash and a roll of poop bags. Carry enough kibble for a small meal or two, a chew toy, and a water bottle and collapsible bowl in case you find yourself stranded at an airport.

Clearing security

It's good to be prepared for what will happen when you and your dog approach the security check. Rover is not exempt from a security screening – but don't worry, he won't be forced through the X-ray machine!

The security officers will indicate what they expect from you, but there's a good chance they'll ask you to remove your dog from his carrier so he can walk (or be carried) through the metal detector with you, while the carrier goes on the belt to be X-rayed.

Arrive at the airport with plenty of time to pass security and get to your gate – you don't want to be rushed. Keep your carry-on baggage to a minimum so you can focus on handling your dog at the checkpoint, and put everything on the belt before you take him out of the carrier. Make sure you have a leash with you, and be alert to your dog's behavior – even calm dogs can get nervous and scared in an unfamiliar environment surrounded by strangers.

If Rover is flying in the hold

If you have a larger dog or are flying on an airline that doesn't permit cabin travel, your dog will fly in the hold, as part of your checked baggage. While it may make you nervous to be separated from Rover for the duration of the flight, the important thing to know is that pets in the hold are in a pressurized, temperature-controlled environment with plenty of oxygen. He should be comfortable there. The hold will be dimly lit – Rover won't be in complete darkness. He'll feel and hear much the same as what we do in the cabin – but with much more legroom!

Choose a pet-friendly airline with a good safety record and, for additional peace of mind, check when you book exactly what conditions your pooch will experience in the hold.

Your dog as cargo

Yes, your pooch is more precious than cargo! But some experts recommend transporting dogs as cargo (ie in the hold of a plane that you're not flying on) as a safer option than bringing him as your checked baggage.

If he flies as cargo, your dog will be checked in at the airline's cargo facility, where employees are trained to handle live animals safely. Pet-friendly airlines will ensure that pets are last on and first off, so they're not left to sit on the tarmac, and they'll be transported in temperature-controlled vehicles.

This mode of transport tends to be more expensive, especially if you have a bigger dog, as freight price is based on weight. It will generally need to be handled by a shipping agent, which adds to the cost – but will significantly reduce your hassle, and increase your peace of mind.

Using a pet shipping agent

Some airlines require you to book your pet, whether as checked baggage or as cargo, through a particular pet shipping service that they have an arrangement with to organize pet travel. Even if this isn't the case for the airline you're traveling with, it can be a good idea to let experienced professionals take care of your dog's transport, especially if there are connections or quarantine regulations at your destination.

Be sure you use a professional pet shipper who's a member of IPATA (International Pet and Animal Transportation Association). Get in touch with them well in advance, especially for international travel. The services they offer will vary, but most of them should:

• **Provide expert advice on getting your dog ready to travel, including quarantine and customs requirements at your destination.**
• **Make sure your dog has all the vaccinations and treatments he needs.**
• **Prepare all the necessary documentation.**

• **Choose the right crate for your dog's size and deliver it to your home.**
• **Give your dog a health check before the flight.**

Choosing a crate

Another good reason to consider using a pet shipping agent is the strict rules regarding how pets must be crated for transport. The International Air Transport Association (IATA) has extensive guidelines available at the 'pet's corner' of their website (www. iata.org/whatwedo/cargo/live-animals/pets). Only some of those are listed below – if you're organizing your dog's transport yourself, be sure that your crate fulfills all requirements.

• **The crate must be large enough for your dog to stand, turn around, and lie down in comfortably.**

Pooch-friendly airports

It's happy days for doggy travel if you're flying within (or to) the US. In 2009 a federal mandate was passed requiring that airports provide 'pet relief areas' to cater for service animals and growing volumes of pet flyers. The result? Airports across the US are attempting to outdo each other in a dog-friendliness arms race of artificial grass and plastic fire hydrants.

The airports listed below are some of the best. Be aware that in most cases the pet areas are outside the security checkpoints.

Denver International Airport is home to the 'Paradise 4 Paws' resort, featuring private suites with flat-screen TVs and a bone-shaped pool. Your dog can board for day or overnight stays, enjoying grooming, massages, and obedience classes.

Atlanta International Airport boasts a fenced, off-leash outdoor dog park, complete with benches, rocks and even dog-inspired sculptures!

Philadelphia International Airport has no fewer than seven outdoor 'Pet Ports,' ranging in size from 250 to 600 sq ft (23–55 sq m).

JFK International Airport, New York is upping the ante with 'The Ark,' its US$48 million animal-shipping terminal including a 20,000-sq-ft (1900-sq-m) dog resort. Rover can stay in 5-bone luxury, with bone-shaped pools, massages, and 'pawdicures'.

• It must be made of fiberglass, metal, rigid plastic, metal mesh, solid wood, or plywood (but note that some airlines don't accept wooden crates), sturdy in design, and not collapsible.

• The floor must be solid and leak-proof.

• The long side of the crate must have handles.

• It must have ventilation on at least two sides for domestic flights, and four sides for international flights.

• Water and food bowls must be attached to the inside of the front door and be refillable from the outside of the crate.

Preparing the crate

As well as making sure your crate fulfills IATA and airline requirements, you'll want to make sure Rover feels safe and comfortable there. The most important thing is that he is accustomed to it and has positive associations with it (see p14 for how to crate-train your dog).

• Line the crate with an absorbent pad or soft bedding, and place a favorite soft toy, blanket, or something with your scent on it inside.

• The crate must display 'Live Animal' stickers on the outside – affix these plus your own identification stickers. Write something like 'I'm Rover and I'm very friendly!' to put baggage handlers at ease and draw attention to the precious cargo inside.

• Attach a plastic sleeve containing copies of your pet's veterinary certificate, your contact information and the details of your journey.

• The day before the flight, fill the water dish and freeze it. Attach it to the inside of the crate just before you check the dog in.

- **Prepare a couple of durable treat-dispensing toys to place in the crate, too.**
- **Attach a small zip-lock bag of kibble to the outside of the crate, so your dog can be fed if the flight is delayed.**

Flying healthy

Visit your vet before you fly so they can assess your dog's health and make sure his vaccinations, worming and flea and tick treatments are up-to-date.

Get it in writing

Some airlines request a health certificate for your dog to fly – not all do, but all require that your dog is healthy to travel, so it's safest to have proof on hand.

In the US, many states require a health certificate (called a Certificate of Veterinary Inspection) that has been issued within ten days of travel. It is only good for 30 days after your vet signs it, and both ends of your journey need to be covered, so if your trip lasts longer than 30 days, you'll need to get another one at your destination.

Hot dogs...

Pets won't be accepted by most airlines if the temperature is above 84°F (29°C) at any location on your itinerary – including departure point, arrival point, and any layovers (it's 75°F / 24°C for snub-nosed dogs). Many airlines impose a blanket embargo during summer months when temperatures are likely to be high.

The risk to Rover is not in the hold, where the temperature is controlled, but in the holding area where it may not be, or when he is sitting on the tarmac waiting to be loaded.

If traveling in the summer is unavoidable, choose a flight that leaves after dark and arrives early morning before the runway begins to heat up. Some airlines are more flexible than others – talk to them about their rules. They may still accept your dog at these times, even if their embargo is technically in effect.

...and pupsicles

Pets won't be accepted when the ground temperature is below 45°F (7°C) at any location on your itinerary, unless you have a veterinarian's statement of low temperature acclimatization, which your vet may be willing to issue if you have a long-haired or thick-coated dog accustomed to cold temperatures. Not all airlines accept these certificates, but it's worth making enquiries.

Short-nosed dogs

Boxers, pugs, bulldogs, Pekinese, and similar dogs, known as snub-nosed or, more scientifically, brachycephalic breeds, are more sensitive to climate and pressure changes. Flying is more risky for them due to their shortened respiratory systems. Airlines usually have specific regulations for transporting these breeds (particularly during hot or cold weather); for example, almost no US airlines allow any type of bulldog to travel in the hold. These regulations differ between airlines and are subject to change – check with the airline and discuss with your vet the specific risk to your squish-nosed pooch.

Your dog's age

Puppies' respiratory systems take some time to become fully formed. Most airlines require your dog to be at least eight weeks old before he can fly. It is best to wait until the dog's first vaccinations are given at 10-12 weeks (and note that for international travel, rabies vaccinations are generally not given until 12 weeks).

Should you sedate your dog?

While you might choose to pop a sleeping pill for the flight, the experts – including the American Veterinary Medical Association (AVMA) – agree: *don't* sedate your dog for air travel.

In an aircraft at altitude, the effects of drugs are unpredictable, and they may be enhanced. It's thought that dogs' natural ability to balance is altered under sedation, so when the crate is moved, the dog may not be able to brace itself to prevent injury. And the risk of respiratory and cardiovascular problems may be increased, particularly for snub-nosed dogs.

Although your dog may be excitable on the trip to the airport and during loading, he will probably settle down to rest in the darkened cargo hold and be in no need of sedation to cope with the flight.

Top tips for flying with Rover

Book early – most airlines have a limited number of dog spaces. Don't buy your own ticket until you're sure there's space (either in the cabin or the hold) for your pooch.

Try to fly direct to avoid the additional stress of unloading and reloading Rover – both to him and to you – especially if he's traveling in the hold. Who hasn't lost checked baggage between flight connections? And of course, look for the shortest possible flight time.

Identify your dog in as many ways as possible! He should, of course, be microchipped. Your crate or carrier should be clearly labeled with your details. Purchase a nylon safety or breakaway collar and write your details right on the collar – don't attach tags as these can get snagged on the crate's wire door.

Tape a photo of your dog to the outside of his crate, and carry one with you onto the plane. If he becomes lost in transit, the photos will make it easier for the search party to find him.

On flight day, feed him about four hours before the flight, if possible, and make sure he's well exercised before getting into his crate or carrier. Continue to give him water right up to the time of travel.

Time your arrival at the airport carefully – you want to have enough time to give Rover water and a chance to pee, but avoid having him wait too long in the airport or on the tarmac. Check (and double-check) the airline's check-in opening and closing times.

Tell the pilot if possible, and certainly the flight crew, that your dog is in the hold. You might even want to make a gesture – give them some chocolates and a photo of your dog with a note introducing you both – that will ensure they have you (and Rover) in mind in the event of any complications on your flight.

Have a back-up plan in case your dog is refused at the airport due to a reservation mix-up, extreme weather, etc.

Be confident, calm and happy when you check in and say goodbye to your crated dog.

If your dog needs to pee when traveling in the cabin, take him to the bathroom, lay a pee pad on the floor, and urge him to go (if your dog doesn't know how to use a pee pad, start training him now!)

Riding the Rails

Traveling by train can be a great alternative to driving or, especially, flying – having your pooch on the floor beside you is far preferable to storing him in a plane's cargo hold!

Depending on where you're traveling, warm welcomes for woofers can be harder to find on the train, compared to the increasingly dog-friendly skies. In the USA you may struggle to get where you want to go. But in the pooch's paradise of Europe, train travel is super-fast, very comfortable, and remarkably dog-friendly. A multi-country European jaunt avec Rover? Totally doable.

Research thoroughly and reset your travel dial to 'slow and leisurely' – it's about the journey, not just the destination, right? Consider planning a more gentle, old-fashioned journey, where you and your furry friend can relax into the tempo of life on the rails.

In the USA

First, the bad news. Amtrak, the only cross-country train system in the USA, allows only service dogs – if you're just friends, he's not welcome.

But there's a light at the end of that tunnel. Since 2014 Amtrak has been running a government mandated carry-on pet pilot program that's expected to move the system closer to pet friendliness.

At the time of writing, the program was running only on limited train services, and only for pets in carriers measuring 19in (48cm) long by 14in (36cm) wide and 10.5in (27cm) high. However, the program has expanded since its inception and with luck will eventually result in cross-country services that welcome all our furry friends. For more info, see www.amtrak.com/carry-on-pets.

State by state

Happily, many smaller regional rail lines are more welcoming. But sadly for great Dane – or even golden retriever – owners, it's rare for dogs bigger than carrier-sized to be allowed on public transport.

There are no hard-and-fast rules – carefully check the regulations for the area you'll be traveling in, and don't expect the rules for neighboring or even overlapping authorities to be consistent. Most transit authorities cover pet regulations on their websites. There are some notably dog-friendly jurisdictions:

• **San Francisco's BART** allows pets in carriers at no additional charge, but no dogs on leashes.
• **In Seattle and King County** dogs on leashes can ride at the discretion of the driver, as long as they are well behaved and sit on the floor (or your lap). Bigger

dogs have to buy a ticket (or have you buy one for them).

• **In Boston** you can take large, leashed dogs on the T during off-peak hours.

• **New York's subway** (and the Long Island Railroad) allows pets in 'kennels or similar containers' that can be held on your lap.

• **Chicago's** transit authority allows pets in small containers that fit on your lap around Chicago, but not on the commuter rail service between Chicago and northeastern Illinois.

• **Maryland**, West Virginia, and Washington D.C.'s MARC allows small pets in carriers.

In Canada

On Via Rail, the national passenger network, pets aren't allowed to mingle with humans – they travel in the baggage car. That mans they can only travel on trains with a checked baggage service. Also, because baggage cars are often heated but not air-conditioned, pets aren't carried at all from June 1 to September 22, due to lack of ventilation. (The Montréal–Halifax service, which has air-conditioned cargo cars, offers year-round pet transport.)

In Europe

Once again, we turn to Europe to find dogs roaming freely throughout the land without restriction (with one exception – see opposite). The train travel rules within most countries are dog-friendly, and thanks to the EU Pet Travel Scheme, it's easy for dogs to country-hop.

The main thing to remember when you're roving the EU with Rover is that he needs to have his papers in order – that means an EU pet passport. Even if you

Crossing the English Channel with Rover

If you're planning a European jaunt with your dog: he's not allowed on the Eurostar. This train, which travels under the English Channel, is the easiest way to get from the UK to the continent, so it's a pity for dog-lovers that Rover's not welcome!

But there are other options. Here's a snapshot, but for the full lowdown visit the internet's premier trainspotter, the Man in Seat 61 (www.seat61.com).

London to Amsterdam by train and ferry

Catch the Dutch Flyer, an integrated, overnight train and ferry service from London to Amsterdam. The ferry has on-board kennels (and en suite cabins for the humans). From Amsterdam, hop on an onward train to other points around Europe.

London to Paris by train and taxi

Take a domestic UK train from London to Folkestone (dogs travel free). At Folkestone jump in a taxi (book ahead) which will go on the Eurotunnel car shuttle train to Calais. From there, take a domestic French train to Paris.

London to Paris by train and ferry

Catch a domestic UK train to Newhaven, then a DFDS ferry across the Channel from Newhaven to Dieppe. Most ferry companies don't allow passengers to take pets; DFDS does, as long as they're in a crate. Your dog is handed to staff at check-in and returned to you after the crossing. From Dieppe, take a domestic French train to Paris.

don't need to cross borders, it's required as proof that your dog is fit to travel. Carry it with you or risk being fined and thrown off the train!

• **In the UK** up to two dogs can travel with you free of charge on all trains, as long as they don't endanger or inconvenience those around you. They must be on a leash at all times (unless in a carrier), and mustn't take up a seat (or there may be a fee).

• **In France** dogs are welcome on all trains, *bien sûr*. Small dogs (under 13lbs or 6kg) in carriers pay no more than around €5 per journey; larger dogs on leashes pay half the full second class fare (even if traveling in first class). It's a similar story in **Switzerland.**

• **On Dutch trains**, a small dog in a carrier or on your lap is free of charge; a larger dog on a leash needs a 'dog day-ticket' (Dagkaart Hond) for around €3.

• **In Italy** dogs can travel on trains, either in a carrier or on a leash (and sometimes muzzled). Specific rules and charges vary from service to service – see trenitalia.com for details.

• **In Spain**, dogs under 22lbs (10kg) can travel in a carrier, but larger dogs aren't allowed on trains.

• **On German trains** small dogs in carriers go free and larger dogs pay the child rate. Note that breeds classed as 'dangerous' aren't allowed on trains.

In Australia

The rules are different wherever you go. In Melbourne, you can bring your dog on the train whether he's in a carrier or on a leash, but on regional Victorian trains he must be in a carrier. In Sydney and NSW, animals aren't allowed on trains at all. Plan ahead and check the rules for the areas you'll be traveling in.

Doggy train etiquette

• As for any carrier, make sure it has a leak-proof bottom, is well ventilated, and is big enough that that your dog is comfortable.

• If your dog is on a leash, keep him very close to you and make him sit quietly. Don't let him block doorways or thoroughfares.

• If your dog needs to be muzzled, make sure that he's used to it by practicing with him before your trip.

• Of course, you must clean up any mess your dog creates (minimize the risk of this by ensuring he's well toileted before you go to the train – it's not a position you want to be in!)

• Don't choose peak commuting times to travel. It's easy to forget when you're on a vacation time-table, but the rest of the world is on 9–5. It will be more challenging to negotiate a crowded carriage.

• Keep your dog happy. You know him best – whether it takes treats or a favorite toy, make sure he has something to keep him calm and occupied.

• If your dog is traveling in his carrier, it's safer to keep him in there as you arrive at the station and go to the platform. Think about it from your dog's point of view: a strange crowded space with new sounds and smells – and then the approach of a loud rumbling beast! Don't risk your dog getting spooked and darting unpredictably.

• Try to find a space at the edge of the carriage where you won't be crowded by standing passengers. Move if a neighboring passenger complains of being allergic. And if your dog gets agitated and whiny, consider getting off early to calm him down.

Dog-friendly
places to stay

Whether you're planning a camping adventure or a big-city jaunt, where to stay is one of your biggest decisions. And traveling with a pooch is going to change your accommodation equation.

But it need not be a limiting factor. Pet travel is big business, and more and more hotel and motel chains, campgrounds, and private B&Bs are chasing the doggy dollar. You may have to do a bit more research, but whatever your destination, you should be able to find lodgings that both meet your human needs and welcome your furry companion. Just be prepared to look harder, cast your net more widely and be flexible about the human amenities.

Here's some advice on your options. For suggested online resources that will help you find the perfect kennel-sweet-kennel, see p109.

Hotels and motels

It's becoming increasingly common for hotels to put out the welcome mat for four-legged guests, especially in the US. Elsewhere, individual hotels in a chain may be dog friendly, but you're less likely to find a chain like The Kimpton (see p93) where they're panting to attract the pooch market. Wherever you're looking, the popularity of pet travel means that most places will specify their pet policy on their website.

Your search is also made easier by the fact that most of the big hotel booking sites like Agoda, Expedia and Wotif allow you to filter your search by 'pets allowed' – even if you don't plan to book through those sites, it's a great place to start your search so you can narrow down your options.

Another way to save searching time is to use a pet-specific directory like BringFido.com (for the US and Canada) or dogfriendlybritain.co.uk (for the UK and Ireland). If you're looking for something luxe, thejet-setpets.com has top-notch options all over the world, and you can browse the pet-friendly collection on the Mr & Mrs Smith website for boutique doggy digs.

Look for places that go out of their way to call out their dog-friendly accomplishments – a 'pet friendly' page on the website is a good start. Hotels that allow pets generally have a limited number of pet-friendly rooms that may book out early. As with everything else on your doggy holiday, start planning well ahead.

B&Bs and private properties

The beauty of small, privately-run accommodations is that the owners create their own personal ambiance, and if you find a B&B run by dog-lovers, it can be

the perfect place for you and your furry friend. Often these lodgings are dog-friendly because the owners have their own dogs on-site, so Rover will have instant friends.

TripAdvisor is particularly useful for finding such treasures – you can filter by B&B and by 'pets allowed', and read user reviews which will give you a clue as to how dog-friendly the place really is. Again, even if you'd rather make your booking directly with the owners, this kind of site is unbeatable for discovering fantastic possibilities you may not have known existed.

You'll also find specialist websites like www.holiday cottages.co.uk (for stand-alone lodgings in the UK) where dog-friendliness is the default setting: you have to choose to filter dogs out! You can specify whether there are one, two or three dogs in your party.

The sharing economy is revolutionizing travel accommodations. Sites like Airbnb, VRBO and HomeAway allow you to connect directly with people who want to rent out their home, or part of their home. Like privately run B&Bs, the proprietors alone set their policy on pets. The real boon for dog-loving travelers is access to self-contained accommodation, perhaps with outside space, where you and Rover can do your own thing without bothering anyone else. You can also get access to off-the-tourist-track areas where there is no formal tourist accommodation available, but which are close to a dog park or beach.

This revolution is still in progress and in some countries the legal position of these businesses is still under a question mark. There are also untested legal areas, like liability if things go wrong. Do some research and be sure that you're comfortable with how it all works.

Campgrounds and holiday parks

While these can be some of the dog-friendliest places around, be aware that not all campgrounds allow dogs. Often, your pooch won't be welcome at campgrounds located within national parks (which many countries forbid dogs from entering altogether).

The best way to find camping spots is often by state-based or regional websites, which usually have a 'pets allowed' filter. BringFido.com is a great resource for finding campgrounds all over the US and Canada. Pitchup.com is a great site for finding a place to pitch a tent or park a caravan all over the UK and Europe. In Australia, the Big4 chain has many pet-friendly holiday parks (www.big4.com.au), and www.exploreaustralia.net.au is good for finding out which campsites are dog friendly (generally, camping in national parks is a no-no, but state forests and other parks are OK).

Questions to ask when booking

• **Are there restrictions on particular breeds, or size limits? Some accommodations only welcome dogs under a certain size.**

• **Is there a fee? The nightly hotel rate for doggy guests is around US$25, rising depending on the luxury of the lodgings. Some places may request a refundable cleaning deposit. In others, there is no charge. Know in advance to avoid sticker shock.**

• **Do you need proof of vaccination? Some places will request this – even if not, it's good practice to always take it with you when you travel.**

• **Will you be allowed to leave your dog alone in your room? Some hotels forbid this, or will ask that you crate your dog if you have to leave. Dog-friendly places should have recommendations for local day-care or dog-walking services.**

• If you're staying at a campground or resort, ask how big the grounds are and whether dogs are allowed off-leash. If it's a hotel, where is the nearest off-leash park? You want to know there's some open space close by for easily accessible romping.

• What special amenities are offered? See below for details on what to expect from pooch-loving lodgings.

• If you're staying at a B&B or private accommodation, find out how secure the property is. Is there sufficient perimeter fencing so your dog can roam free in the garden or backyard?

• When you're booking a hotel stay, request a ground-floor room near an entrance or exit, which will make unloading and loading – as well as potty breaks – much easier.

Doggy welcome baskets – and more

What should you expect from your dog-friendly lodging? The ante is constantly being upped, as the top end of the market finds new ways to get tails wagging – though many of the flourishes seem targeted directly at doting humans.

The basics for a pet-friendly hotel in the US include:

• Bedding, food and water bowls for your room (the doggier the lodging, the plusher the bedding).

• Complimentary poop bags at the front desk.

• Information about local vets, groomers, dog-friendly restaurants and dog parks.

• A 'welcome basket' with doggy snacks and treats in your room.

• Warm welcomes, pats and smiles from the staff.

There are plenty of places that go above and beyond in making you and your dog feel special. Some places offer a special doggy in-room service menu with deliciously human-sounding choices like filet mignon and chicken pot pie, and all-natural organic treats are a popular inclusion in doggy welcome baskets. Pampered pooches might enjoy an in-room massage, 'pawdicure,' or 'Rover reiki.'

Countryside resorts might offer appealing dog-and-owner group activities like a 'hike for hounds.' Our favorite? For more independent dogs, Loews Coronado in southern California offers a canine surfing lesson, complete with doggy board shorts or bandana and a surf 'n' turf meal for your intrepid four-legged travel friend.

The world's dog-friendliest hotels

There's dog friendly, and then there's Kimpton. This US boutique hotel chain allows not only dogs (of any size), but any pet you can fit into the lobby, of unlimited number. For free.

Of course you'll expect designer doggy beds and a VIP (Very Important Pet) welcome basket with bowls and treats. Your concierge will advise you on all the local canine hotspots, and organize dog minding, grooming, and walking services.

At some Kimpton properties you'll be welcomed by a 'Director of Pet Relations.' In Portland, Oregon that's Daphne, an Australian shepherd and Labrador retriever mix, and at Alexandria, Virginia, the role is filled by Charlie, an energetic bichon frise. In San Diego, Posh, a pampered Jack Russell, provides a guide to her favorite local attractions. Your pooch can get to know his host at the nightly wine reception (aka 'Yappy Hour').

In Philadelphia (Director of Pet Relations: Dexter the cockapoo) they run the 'Palomar Pet Pals' program. Adoptable dogs from a local shelter hang out in the lobby, spreading doggy love to travel-hassled, newly arrived guests and playing social butterfly during Yappy Hour.

And if you're traveling dog-free and feeling bereft, there's 'Guppy Love', a goldfish in your room to keep you company. Don't worry – the staff will feed it for you.

You made it! The hard part is over, you and Rover have reached your destination, and it's time for some doggy fun.

First, help him settle in to his new environment, whether it's a campground, resort, apartment, or hotel room. Take it slow and keep an eye on him to be sure he's adjusting well.

As you enjoy your vacation, your pooch's tail will be wagging just to be doing whatever you're doing. But be sure you make some time for dog fun. Whether it's dog parks, beach trips, or neighborhood walks, make sure Rover gets lots of stimulation and exercise.

If you can't take him with you when you visit that museum or have dinner at a fancy restaurant, make sure he's well looked after.

Helping him settle in

You're on vacation! And while it's exciting (now that the stress of getting here is over) and you want to get out and start exploring, consider that Rover might need a bit more time to get accustomed to his new surrounds.

Travel can be stressful for dogs, and your pooch may feel unsure about his new environment. Some dogs readily absorb their owners' emotions: if you feel hyped-up or scattered, he may be jumpy or feel insecure. Your dog may become focused on establishing his new territory, or he may want to stay in his crate or hide under the bed.

Be attuned to your dog. What signs is he showing? Is he acting unusually? Be prepared to take things slower than you otherwise would to ensure that you're not rushing him into feeling comfortable in these strange surrounds.

Decide on an area for him. Dogs feel secure when they have their own special place. Put his bedding (or crate) there, some favorite toys or chews, and introduce him to the space. It should be somewhere you can close off, so he can be confined to this dog-safe area if you're out without him.

Before taking him outside for the first time, check the boundary fencing and make sure the area is secure before letting him off the leash.

Take him outside often at first so he learns where to do his business. If he does have an accident indoors, remember the rules of puppy toilet training: be patient, don't get angry or punish him, and quietly clean up the mess. Praise him when he goes to the toilet where he's supposed to.

Stick to your usual routines as much as possible – this will help him to settle.

Dogville, USA

Fancy a big-city break, stateside? Choose one of these poochified cities and enjoy an urban adventure with your furry traveling companion.

Austin, Texas

Austin's pro-pooch attitude (and the temperate climate, allowing year-round outdoor dining) makes it a doggy paradise. Most restaurants have patios and welcome your dog. Best of all are the sprawling neighborhood bars that double as off-leash parks. Or maybe they're dog parks with bars attached – either way, they're a top spot for you and your canine companion.

San Francisco, California

There's an urban legend that dogs outnumber children in the City by the Bay. True or not, woofers are well catered for with lots of off-leash parks and beautiful dog-friendly beaches. San Fran is perfectly compact for on-foot, on-leash exploration. If you need help with the hills, MUNI cable cars, trams and buses allow dogs of all sizes.

Seattle, Washington

Seattle is so dog-friendly that some restaurants allow you to bring your pooch inside, French-style. There are lots of city pooch parks (including indoor parks, to cater for the city's renowned raininess), and great hiking trails around the surrounding mountains and lakes. You can take dogs of all sizes on all public transport, and on many of the lake cruises. They're welcome at the famous Pike Place Market – and even inside some of the shops.

Portland, Oregon
There are over 30 off-leash parks to romp through. To wind down, enjoy a local brew while Rover makes new friends in the beer garden of one of four Lucky Labrador Brewing Company locations. Most of the stores in the downtown Pearl District welcome doggy shoppers, with water bowls out front and treats inside. Pooches are also welcome at the Rose Gardens and the Saturday outdoor market.

Chicago, Illinois
Lake Michigan has 18 miles (29km) of paved trails you can walk with your pooch, and Montrose Beach is the perfect spot for swimming and off-leash romps. Dogs are welcome on the patio of the Bad Dog Tavern – get him to strike a pose and you can submit a photo to the doggy wall of fame. Mercury Cruises run a weekend canine cruise so you can hit the Windy City waterways with your woofer.

If he seems anxious, don't over-soothe as this can reinforce that there's something to be worried about. Be calm and relaxed, and give him as much affection as usual.

Try not to leave him alone for the first little while – 24 to 48 hours if possible. Take him for short walks to help him get used to his new neighborhood. Don't let him off the leash in a strange place unless you're a hundred percent sure he'll respond to your call, or the area is fully fenced.

Finding fun for Rover

Of course, you brought your pooch on vacation so you could have fun with him, and he'll love spending quality time with his best friend – you. Whether you're going on short hikes, day visits to tourist sites or exploring your local area, take him with you whenever you can.

Be aware of the pace you're setting. You know how to read your dog: observe closely and be sure not to push him too hard when you're out exploring. With some dogs you'll be the one struggling to keep up; with others you might need to stop for rest breaks more often than you'd like. But when you're traveling with your pooch, his needs come first.

Your human trip itinerary aside, get out there for some dog-centered fun where both of you can socialize (especially if it's just the two of you on your trip). You know best how social your dog is, but most dogs need a regular butt-sniff, wrestle or friendly romp to stay happy.

Do your research so you can find local dog parks, and even though your thoughts are far from the nine-to-five, time your visits for weekends and the peak hours before and after work so you have the best

chance to meet lots of dogs. Tap into the wealth of local tips that local dog lovers will be only too willing to share about awesome dog-friendly walks, that local pub with a dog-welcoming outdoor area, a great local dog-minder… Dog parks are a goldmine of information, especially useful if you're staying for a longer visit.

Taking it to the next level

What better time than on vacation to try something new? Or maybe your dog is already a pro and you want to keep him in form when you travel. There's a big world of dogs out there, with owners who are constantly sniffing out new ways to amuse themselves and their pooches. Do some online research to find local groups practicing these activities (www.dogplay. com is a good place to start), and tap into a whole new world of doggy adventure.

Flying disc dog sport You might know it as 'Frisbee in the park with Rover,' but it's actually an organized sport with chapters all over the US (and in many other countries, too). While the basics are simple – you throw disc, dog catches disc, dog returns disc – there is plenty of room for creativity, teamwork, and impressive displays of athleticism. The great thing for traveling dogs is that equipment is minimal and it can be done almost anywhere.

Agility is a kind of adventure playground for dogs, where they navigate through an obstacle course of tunnels, jumps, suspended hoops, poles, and platforms. It takes some training, and is great for very active dogs (though almost any dog can participate at some level). There are agility groups and trainers all over, whether Rover wants to get involved or just go along to watch.

Herding is an instinct that has been bred into many of our pet pooches, and it's increasingly popular for owners of non-working dogs to give them exposure to livestock to help preserve the breed's abilities – and give their pooches a buzz. It's a serious competition, but there are also organized 'herding instinct tests' which give an accessible introduction to dogs who might not otherwise have the opportunity – see www.herdingontheweb.com for more information.

Dog-powered sports like skijoring, bikejoring, and rollerjoring (where the dog pulls along its human on skis, bicycle or rollerblades) and canicross (where the human just runs) can be great for dogs over 35 lbs (16kg), especially those who naturally get a kick out of pulling. And great for their owners along for the ride! Some equipment (harnesses) and training is needed to keep you connected and get you working as a team.

Dog camps If these activities sound like fun, why not try them all (and more) at a dog camp? These vacations are custom-made for dogs and their owners, set up to strengthen your relationship with your dog. Many will offer seminars for you on subjects like training techniques, dog behavior, and canine nutrition, and lots of activities for Rover to try – earthdog, 'doga,' coursing, tracking, and water work. Freestyle dance and 'Doglish as a second language'? Why not!

When you can't take him with you

Make sure you've done your research on boarding kennels with day rates in the area. Be organized and contact them well in advance of when you want to go out without Rover, so you can be sure to get a place for him – especially during peak vacation times.

Finding doggy love online

Want to set your dog up on a playdate while you're away? A plethora of doggy social networks and matchmaking apps have come and, mostly, gone. (Research says that less than 0.01 percent of mobile apps are financially successful, so even in the lucrative pet market, the huge majority of startups end up in the doghouse.)

There are still plenty out there – like MatchPuppy, DogDate, Meet My Dog, Sniffr (that's Tinder for dogs) – but despite the adorableness of the concept, like all social networks, until they reach a critical mass of other users their usefulness is limited.

That's not to say you can't find a date for your dog online. Meetup.com – a local networking site with over 24 million members across the globe – lets anyone organize a get-together for any interest, from sport lovers and language learners to singles with social anxiety. Naturally, local dog-walking groups abound. The beauty of Meetup.com is that groups are often hyper-local, so you might be able to find a dog-walking group that meets right near you.

Another good bet is to use your regular social networks to set you and your pooch up for holiday fun times. If you're a member of a breed-based Facebook group, you already have a wide network of people wanting to introduce their dog to yours. Favorite dog blogs or doggy Instagram or Twitter accounts may also present the opportunity to turn virtual friendships into real-world dog dates.

There are web-based dog-minding services springing up all over, where you can find local dog lovers offering dog-minding and doggy day-care – like an Airbnb for dogs. This is often cheaper than a boarding kennel, and your dog will be in a real home. Often you'll be able to read a profile and reviews of the person who'll be looking after him. Do keep in mind that there is a similar level of risk as with other web-based services. Most of the time things go fine, but if they don't you're unlikely to have much recourse.

If he's accustomed to being left alone for long periods (ie while you're at work), if he has settled in well to his new surrounds, and if your accommodation is amenable, comfortable, and safe (for example, a house rental), you could leave him alone. Make sure he has plenty of water and chews or toys to keep him happy. (Note that if you're staying in a hotel or motel, you may not be permitted to do this.)

For more information

Everything for doggy travel

www.bringfido.com Destination guides, airline dog policies, lodging, and attractions worldwide (but especially the USA and Canada)

www.yourdogholidays.co.uk Dog-friendly regional guides and dog travel advice for the UK, plus accommodations listings

www.dogfriendly.com In-depth destination guides for US cities, national parks, beaches, and more. They also publish dog-friendly accommodations guide-books for the USA and Canada

www.gopetfriendly.com Tips, accommodations, sights – everything dog travel

Good advice (and a great read)

www.dogjaunt.com Sensible advice on dog travel (US and international) from a passionate Seattle-based dog owner

www.thebark.com A great doggy journal with an extensive collection of travel-related articles – just enter 'travel' in search

www.dogster.com/topic/dogster-travel Tips and articles on all things dog travel

www.dogtime.com/reference/dog-travel News and tips from the world of dog travel

www.cesarsway.com/dog-care/travel Plenty of advice about training and getting your dog travel-ready, plus tips for safe travel

International travel resources

www.pettravel.com One-stop pet travel shop with details of vaccination and quarantine regulations worldwide, airline policies and many other aspects of international travel. They prepare pet passport packs and provide pet transport

www.gov.uk/take-pet-abroad Rules for dogs travelling to and from the UK and within Europe

www.agriculture.gov.au/cats-dogs Bringing your dog into Australia

www.cdc.gov/importation Bringing your dog to the US; see 'Bringing an animal into the US'

www.mpi.govt.nz/importing Bringing your dog into New Zealand; see 'Live Animals'

Flying dogs and pet-shipping services

www.pettravel.com/passports_container_requirements.cfm Full details, with diagrams of exactly what kind of travel carrier you need

www.barkpost.com/come-fly-with-me A handy summary of requirements, rules, and costs for dog travel on US airlines

www.ipata.org The International Pet and Animal Transportation Association – make sure the shipper you use is a member

www.iata.org/whatwedo/cargo/live-animals/pets International Air Transport Association 'pet's corner' – regulations for air travel

www.petrelocation.com Worldwide shipping, dog travel advice, and relocation success stories to make you go 'awwww!'

www.pet-express.com Helpful advice, full service, and a handy crate-size calculator

www.jetpets.com.au Behind-the-scenes airport videos to show you what Rover will experience in the cargo hold

Accommodations
Worldwide

www.tripadvisor.com All types of lodging; filter by 'Pets allowed' under 'Amenities'

www.airbnb.com Private property rental; filter by 'Pets allowed' under 'Amenities'

www.vrbo.com Private property rental; filter by 'Pet friendly' under 'Suitability'

www.mrandmrssmith.com Boutique hotels; filter by 'Pet friendly' under 'Facilities'

www.thejetsetpets.com Luxury digs for posh pooches

www.marriott.com Almost 1500 luxury dog-friendly hotels around the world

www.fourseasons.com Many hotels in this high-end chain are pet-friendly

USA and Canada

www.bringfido.com Everywhere dogs are welcome, from high-end hotels to campsites

www.dogfriendly.com State-by-state guides; they also publish doggy travel guidebooks

www.petswelcome.com Plots your route and finds dog-friendly stops along the way

www.lq.com Most La Quinta inns in the US, Canada, and Mexico welcome pooches

www.kimptonhotels.com The ultimate chain for pet-friendliness

www.loewshotels.com Pet-friendly hotels and resorts

www.bestwestern.com Over 1600 of this affordable chain's hotels provides digs for cost-conscious canines
www.fairmont.com Many of these high-end hotels and resorts welcome dogs
www.redroof.com Pets stay free at this economy chain

UK and Europe
www.yourdogholidays.co.uk Dog-friendly digs around the UK
www.dogfriendlybritain.co.uk Hotels, guesthouses, cottages, and campsites
www.holidaycottages.co.uk Charming cottages and country houses; pet-friendly options shown by default
www.britainsfinest.co.uk Luxury lodgings; filter your results by 'Dog friendly'
www.hotels.uk.com/pets Dog-friendly hotels and guesthouses

www.bestwestern.co.uk A huge range of hotels and guesthouses, many pet-friendly
www.sawdays.co.uk Special places in the UK and Europe; filter by 'Pets welcome' under 'Features'

Australia
www.stayz.com.au Private property rental; filter by 'Pet friendly' under 'Holiday type'
www.lovemelovemydog.com.au Dog-friendly private property rental
www.big4.com.au Many Big4 camping and caravan parks are pet-friendly
www.bestwestern.com.au Many Best Western hotels welcome pooches

Peer-to-peer dog minding (aka Airbnb for dogs)

Most of these services offer both longer-term overnight stays and doggy day-care.

USA

www.rover.com
www.care.com
www.petsitusa.com This is not peer-to-peer, but a directory of professional pet-sitters across the US

UK

uk.dogbuddy.com
uk.care.com/pet-care
www.pawshake.co.uk

Australia

www.pawshake.com.au
www.pethomestay.com.au

Dog travel health

www.avma.org See 'Pet care' for advice on traveling with pets from the American Veterinary Medical Association
www.humanesociety.org/animals/resources/tips/pet_first_aid_kit.html How to put together a pet first-aid kit

Our favorite dog blogs

There's nothing as inspirational as discovering the travel experiences of other dogs and their human companions. There are some wonderful dog travel blogs out there, often based on hard-won experience and full of handy tips, and sometimes just plain entertaining. These are our favorites.

www.intrepidpup.com Adventurous tales of roadtripping the USA with Tavish, the Hungarian vizsla

www.phileasdogg.com The super-cute and truly amusing blog of Attlee Common, self-described London mongrel, aka Phileas Dogg, travel journalist

www.thejetsetpets.com/blog All the latest news for pampered pooches traveling at the more luxurious end of the scale

www.montecristotravels.com/blog Montecristo is a long-haired chihuahua who travels Europe debunking myths and preconceptions about small-dog travel and sharing his tips and tricks. He tweets too!

www.untamedtravellers.com Zala, meanwhile, is a 70lb (30kg) Dutch Shepherd who's traveled from France to Thailand. This is a great blog for travelers who want advice about going international with a big dog

www.celebritydachshund.com Follow the adventures – and marvel at the photos – of Crusoe, the celebrity miniature dachshund (who has also penned a *New York Times* bestselling book)

www.puppytales.com.au Plenty of good info, but we love this blog for its gorgeous puppy photography (the blogger is a professional pet-snapper) – plus get dog photo tips and join the weekly photo challenge

www.theroadunleashed.com Join Abby and Chewy on their worldwide travel adventures

www.fidoseofreality.com A well-rounded doggy health and wellness blog with a good serving of useful travel advice *www.alfiesblog.com* Alfie is an Entlebucher mountain dog (previously of London, now a San Francisco resident) who wants to tell you all about his off-leash hiking fun

www.andasmalldog.com The blogger is a pet travel agent – yes, there is such a thing! Follow her on Facebook for up-to-the-minute dog travel news

www.gigigriffis.com The fantastic blog of this nomadic writer includes lots of articles about 'Luna the traveling pooch' – honest, first-hand dog travel experiences

www.pupstyle.com Want to travel in style? Find glamping gear, luxury dog beds and the latest in doggy fashion here

www.youdidwhatwithyourweiner.com Dachshunds and hiking. Need we say more?

Other great resources

www.drivingwithdogs.co.uk Find places for walking dogs all over the UK and France, especially along motorways for doggy driving holidays

www.seat61.com/dogs-by-train.htm Dog-friendly train travel in Europe

www.dogjaunt.com/guides/public-transit-pet-policies A wrap-up of public transit dog policies around the US

www.dogtrekker.com Everything you need to know for dog travel around California

www.wildmountainonline.com Gear for the adventurous dog from backpacks to lifejackets

Forums

www.pettravel.com/forum A big US-based forum covering all aspects of dog travel (including the fun bits)

www.bringfido.com/forum Active dog-specific forum, especially helpful for US travelers

www.tripadvisor.com There's a 'Traveling with Pets' forum at the world's most popular travel advice website

www.australianexplorer.com/forum Plenty of useful advice if you're looking for tips on traveling around Australia with a dog

www.thegreynomads.activeboard.com This site for traveling seniors has an active forum with a Traveling with Pets section, especially helpful for RVers

Index

Notes

Notes

Janine Eberle splits her time between Melbourne and Paris and writes about the things she likes – travel, food and dogs.

Her Irish terrier, Molly, regards any open car door as an invitation to jump straight in, sit up in the passenger seat and look impatient.

Jess Golden spends most of her days in her quiet studio with Martha, her trusty terrier-mix.

Jess has illustrated several books for children including *Snow Dog, Sand Dog* by Linda Joy Singleton and *The Wheels on the Tuk Tuk* by Kabir and Surishtha Sehgal.

When she's not busy drawing and painting, Jess is hiking trails or taking mini road trips with Martha and her husband.

Jess's website is www.jessgolden.com

Happy Travels

Published in July 2016 by
Lonely Planet Publications Pty Ltd
ABN 36 005 607 983
www.lonelyplanet.com
ISBN 978 1 76034 0674
© Lonely Planet 2016
Printed in China
10 9 8 7 6 5 4 3 2 1

Written by Janine Eberle
Illustrated by Jess Golden

Managing Director, Publishing Piers Pickard
Associate Publisher Robin Barton
Editors Alison Ridgway, Jessica Cole
Art Direction Daniel Di Paolo
Designer Hayley Warnham
Layout Designer Wibowo Rusli
Print Production Larissa Frost, Nigel Longuet

Lonely Planet offices

AUSTRALIA
The Malt Store, Level 3, 551 Swanston Street, Carlton 3053, Victoria, Australia
Phone 03 8379 8000
Email talk2us@lonelyplanet.com.au

USA
150 Linden St, Oakland, CA 94607
Phone 510 250 6400
Email info@lonelyplanet.com

UNITED KINGDOM
240 Blackfriars Road, London SE1 8NW
Phone 020 3771 5100
Email go@lonelyplanet.co.uk

MIX
Paper from responsible sources
FSC™ C021741

Paper in this book is certified against the Forest Stewardship Council™ standards. FSC™ promotes environmentally responsible, socially beneficial and economically viable management of the world's forests.